Rookie
National Parks™

Great Smoky Mountains National Park

by Lisa M. Herrington

Content Consultant
Nanci R. Vargus, Ed.D.
Professor Emeritus, University of Indianapolis

Reading Consultant
Jeanne M. Clidas, Ph.D.
Reading Specialist

Children's Press®
An Imprint of Scholastic Inc.

Library of Congress Cataloging-in-Publication Data
Names: Herrington, Lisa M., author.
Title: Great Smoky Mountains National Park/by Lisa M. Herrington.
Description: New York, NY: Children's Press, an imprint of Scholastic Inc., 2018. | Series: Rookie national parks | Includes bibliographical references and index.
Identifiers: LCCN 2016051664| ISBN 9780531233313 (reinforced library binding) | ISBN 9780531239032 (paperback: alkaline paper)
Subjects: LCSH: Great Smoky Mountains National Park (N.C. and Tenn.)—Juvenile literature. | Great Smoky Mountains (N.C. and Tenn.)—Juvenile literature.
Classification: LCC F443.G7 H47 2018 | DDC 976.8/89—dc23
LC record available at https://lccn.loc.gov/2016051664

Produced by Spooky Cheetah Press
Design: Judith Christ-Lafond/Joan Michael

Published in 2018 by Children's Press, an imprint of Scholastic Inc.

Printed in China 62

SCHOLASTIC, CHILDREN'S PRESS, ROOKIE NATIONAL PARKS™, and associated logos are trademarks and/or registered trademarks of Scholastic Inc., 557 Broadway, New York, NY 10012.

1 2 3 4 5 6 7 8 9 10 R 27 26 25 24 23 22 21 20 19 18

Photos ©: cover: Pavlo Vakhrushev/Dreamstime; back cover: Edwin Verin/Dreamstime; 1-2: PCRex/Shutterstock; 3: Judy Kennamer/Dreamstime; 4-5: KenCanning/iStockphoto; 6-7: John D. Simmons/Charlotte Observer/MCT/Getty Images; 8-9: Pavlo Vakhrushev/Dreamstime; 10: Sean Pavone/Dreamstime; 11: Chris Murray/Getty Images; 12-13: James Vallee/Dreamstime; 14: Pat & Chuck Blackley/Alamy Images; 15: alex grichenko/iStockphoto; 16-17: Carol R Montoya/Dreamstime; 18: Brian K. Miller/age fotostock; 19: Bob Colley Photography/Alamy Images; 20-21: W. Drew Senter, Longleaf Photography/Getty Images; 22-23 background: Betty4240/Dreamstime; 23 left: Mark Raycroft/Minden Pictures; 23 right: Donald M. Jones/Minden Pictures; 24-25 background: Floris Van Breugel/Nature Picture Library/Getty Images; 24 top: Danita Delimont/Getty Images; 26-30 background: DavidMSchrader/iStockphoto; 26 top left: Steve Byland/Dreamstime; 26 top center: Musat/iStockphoto; 26 top right: Joel Sartore, National Geographic Photo Ark/Getty Images; 26 bottom left: Nicholas Jr/Getty Images; 26 bottom center: Canon_Bob/iStockphoto; 26 bottom right: MYN/JP Lawrence/NPL/Minden Pictures; 27 top left: Josef Pittner/Shutterstock; 27 top right: Jim Cumming/Shutterstock; 27 bottom left: Dorling Kindersley/Getty Images; 27 bottom center: Brian Hagiwara/Getty Images; 27 bottom right: Wizarts/iStockphoto; 30 top left: Benvie/Nature Picture Library/Getty Images; 30 bottom left: nickkurzenko/iStockphoto; 30 top right: Erastef/Dreamstime; 30 bottom right: golfladi/iStockphoto; 31 top: Kelly vanDellen/Shutterstock; 31 center top: thundor/iStockphoto; 31 bottom: RichardBarrow/iStockphoto; 31 center bottom: KenCanning/iStockphoto; 32: Anthony Knight/Dreamstime.

Maps by Jim McMahon.

Table of Contents

Introduction 5

1. Misty Mountains 9

2. Let's Explore! 12

3. From Past to Present 16

4. Amazing Animals 20

Field Guide 26

Where Is Ranger Red Fox? 28

Wildflower Tracker 30

Glossary 31

Index 32

Facts for Now 32

About the Author 32

Introduction

I am Ranger Red Fox, your tour guide. Are you ready for an amazing adventure in the Great Smoky Mountains?

Welcome to
Great Smoky Mountains
National Park!

The Great Smoky Mountains became a **national park** in 1934. People visit parks like this one to explore nature.

This park is named for the mountains that roll across the land. It lies on the border between North Carolina and Tennessee.

This is the most visited national park in the country. It is easy to see why! People are drawn to its thick forests and gentle streams. They come for its sparkling waterfalls, beautiful wildflowers, and amazing animals.

A llama train passes under Grotto Falls. It is delivering supplies to a guest lodge in the park.

United States

Great Smoky
Mountains
National Park

Tennessee →

North
Carolina

N
W ⊕ E
S

This park
gets more than
10 million visitors
a year.

The Smokies are part of the Appalachian mountain range. The Appalachians run from Canada to Alabama.

8

Chapter 1

Misty Mountains

Can you guess how the Great Smoky Mountains got their name? Look at the fog hanging over the mountain **peaks**. Millions of trees in the area give off water that helps form the fog. From a distance, it looks like smoke. So the mountains are nicknamed "the Smokies."

Talk about big! This park covers more than a half million acres. That is an area almost the size of Rhode Island. Some of the oldest mountains on Earth are here.

Scientists believe the Smokies used to be taller. Wind, water, and ice wore down their peaks over time.

The Smokies have gentler peaks than the mountains in the West.

The Little River in Tennessee is 60 miles (97 kilometers) long. About one-third of it runs through the park.

Chapter 2

Let's Explore!

Most people drive through the park. It has more than 380 miles (612 kilometers) of **scenic** roads.

A popular spot is Clingmans Dome. It is the highest point in the park. Visitors can climb to a tower at the top. It has great views on clear days.

Clingmans Dome is 6,643 feet (2,025 meters) high. That is as tall as a stack of 22 Statues of Liberty!

There is a lot to explore on foot as well. The park is filled with more than 850 miles (1,368 kilometers) of hiking trails. In fall, they will take you through trees bursting with color. In spring and summer, colorful wildflowers bloom. The landscape is dotted with more than 1,500 types of flowering plants.

The Smokies are sometimes called "Wildflower National Park."

rhododendrons

Chapter 3

From Past to Present

Want to travel back in time? You can do that at Cades Cove. It is a **valley** between the mountains. There you will find log cabins, old churches, and mills. They show what life was like for people who lived here long ago.

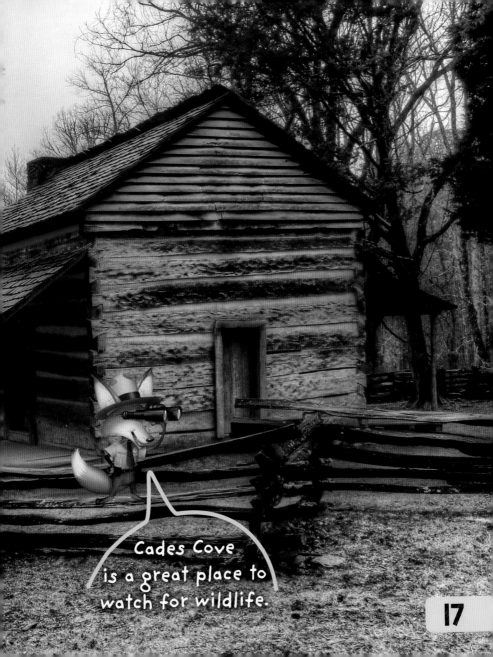

Cades Cove is a great place to watch for wildlife.

Ramsey Cascades is as tall as a 10-story building! The water drops 100 feet (30 meters) into a pool below.

Today, people come to enjoy the mountains in many ways. Visitors fish, bike, and ride horses. They camp under the stars or listen to a quiet stream. They also enjoy the park's many wonderful waterfalls.

Ramsey Cascades is the tallest waterfall in the park.

These fishers may catch trout.

Chapter 4

Amazing Animals

A black bear scurries up a tree. Another searches for acorns and berries to eat. You are in black bear country. More than 1,500 live in the park.

Never approach or try to feed bears!

Black bears usuall ignore humans if the humans keep their distance and ignore them.

Bears are not the only animals found here. Deer, elk, and wild turkeys also roam the woods.

Perhaps the park's most unusual creatures are salamanders. More than 30 kinds live here! They include lungless salamanders.

This park is known as the "Salamander Capital of the World."

Lungless salamanders breathe through their skin.

white-tailed deer

wild turkey

A pileated woodpecker feeds its chicks.

Imagine you could visit the Great Smoky Mountains. What would you do there?

Be sure to bring your binoculars! You can scan the trees for sparrows, woodpeckers, and other birds. You may even notice an owl perched on a branch.

In spring, fireflies put on a dazzling evening display. Thousands flash their lights at the same time! It is just one of the many stunning sights that will leave you in awe of the Great Smoky Mountains.

These are just some of the incredible animals that make their home in the Great Smoky Mountains.

bluebird

beaver

brook trout

flying squirrel

woodpecker

salamander

Wildlife by the Numbers

The park is home to about...

240 types of birds   **65** types of mammals

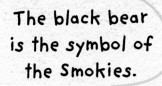

The black bear is the symbol of the Smokies.

elk

white-tailed deer

black bear

great horned owl

wild turkey

82 types of reptiles and amphibians

67 types of fish

Where Is Ranger Red Fox?

Oh no! Ranger Red Fox has lost his way in the park. Use the map and the clues below to find him.

1. Ranger Red Fox started near a log cabin at Cades Cove.

2. He ran south. Then he stopped to smell some wildflowers on the Appalachian Trail.

3. Next, he ran east along the trail to Clingmans Dome. What a view!

4. Finally, he hiked northeast. He ended up near rushing water.

Help! Can you find me?

Great Smoky Mountains National Park

TENNESSEE

Ramsey
Cascades

Cades
Cove

Appalachian
Trail

Clingmans
Dome

Fontana
Lake

NORTH CAROLINA

U.S.
Area of map

Alaska and Hawaii are not drawn to
scale or placed in their proper places.

Compass Rose

North

West ◆ East

South

Wildflower Tracker

**Can you match each wildflower to its name?
Read the clues to help you.**

1. Yellow lady's slipper
Clue: This beautiful orchid has a little pouch, but it's not for your feet.

2. Mountain laurel
Clue: These small cup-shaped flowers grow in groups.

3. Flame azalea
Clue: Their fiery color makes these beautiful blooms stand out.

4. Rhododendron
Clue: These colorful flowers come in different shades, including purple.

A.

B.

C.

D.

Glossary

national park (**nash**-uh-nuhl pahrk): area where the land and its animals are protected by the U.S. government

peaks (**peeks**): pointed tops of mountains

scenic (**see**-nik): having beautiful natural surroundings

valley (**val**-ee): area of low ground between two hills or mountains, usually containing a river

Index

activities 19

animals 6, 20–25

Appalachian Mountain range 8

black bears 20

Cades Cove 16–17

Clingmans Dome 12–13

deer 22

elk 22

fireflies 25

fog 9

forests 6

hiking trials 15

mountains 5, 8-10, 16, 19

nicknames 9, 15, 22

North Carolina 5

owl 25

peaks 9, 10

Ramsey Cascades 19

roads 12

salamanders 22

sparrows 25

streams 6, 19

Tennessee 5

trees 9, 15

waterfalls 6, 19

wildflowers 6, 15

wild turkeys 22

woodpeckers 25

Facts for Now

Visit this Scholastic Web site for more information
on Great Smoky Mountains National Park:
www.factsfornow.scholastic.com
Enter the keywords **Great Smoky Mountains**

About the Author

Lisa M. Herrington has written many books for kids. She loves exploring our country's beautiful national parks. Lisa lives in Connecticut with her husband and daughter.